The
Lyndon
Johnsons

by
Cass R. Sandak

CRESTWOOD HOUSE
New York

Maxwell Macmillan Canada
Toronto

Maxwell Macmillan International
New York   Oxford   Singapore   Sydney

Library of Congress Cataloging-in-Publication Data
Sandak, Cass R.
    The Lyndon Johnsons / by Cass R. Sandak. — 1st ed.
        p. cm. — (First families)
    Includes bibliographical references and index.
    Summary: Examines the life of the thirty-sixth president, with an emphasis on his family relationships and his
years in the White House.
    ISBN 0-89686-644-0
    1. Johnson, Lyndon B. (Lyndon Baines), 1908–1973—Juvenile literature. 2. Johnson, Lady Bird, 1912–
—Juvenile literature. 3. Johnson family—Juvenile literature. 4. Presidents—United States—Biography—Juvenile
literature. 5. Presidents—United States—Wives—Biography—Juvenile literature. 6. United States—Politics and
government—1961–1963—Juvenile literature. 7. United States—Politics and government—1963–1969—Juvenile
literature.[1. Johnson, Lyndon B. (Lyndon Baines), 1908–1973. 2. Johnson, Lady Bird, 1912– . 3. Presidents. 4. First
ladies.] I. Title. II. Series: Sandak, Cass R. First families.
E847.S26   1993
973.923'092—dc20
[B]   92-33522

Photo Credits
Cover: AP—Wide World Photos
AP—Wide World Photos: 4, 7, 9, 11, 12, 16, 17, 20, 25, 27, 31, 32, 35, 41, 42, 43
The Bettmann Archive: 39, 44

Macmillan Publishing Company   Maxwell Macmillan Canada, Inc.
866 Third Avenue   1200 Eglinton Avenue East
New York, NY 10022   Suite 200
                                     Don Mills, Ontario M3C 3N1

CRESTWOOD HOUSE

Macmillan Publishing Company is part of the Maxwell Communication Group of Companies.

Produced by Flying Fish Studio

Printed in the United States of America

First edition

10 9 8 7 6 5 4 3 2 1

Contents

Lyndon B. Johnson is sworn in as President of the United States.

President by Accident

The date was November 22, 1963. It was a Friday afternoon, the week before Thanksgiving. The country was reeling from the news that President John F. Kennedy had just been shot as he rode in a motorcade through downtown Dallas, Texas. Almost everyone who was alive at that time remembers what he or she was doing when the shocking news came.

Lyndon Johnson was the vice president. He and his wife, Lady Bird, had been riding in a separate car, two cars behind the president.

For several hours the news was murky. Then it was announced that an assassin's bullet had killed John F. Kennedy. By late afternoon the presidential plane—Air Force One—was speeding toward Washington, D.C. On it was the body of the slain president, along with his widow, Mrs. Jacqueline Kennedy.

Also on board were the new president, Lyndon B. Johnson, and his wife, the new first lady. By the terms of the Constitution, the vice president automatically became the new president upon the death of the current president. At 2:38 P.M., just before the plane left Dallas's Love Field, Federal District Judge Sarah T. Hughes had sworn Johnson in as the 36th president of the United States. This made it official. The oath itself took just 28 seconds to administer.

Americans braced themselves for the four-day ordeal of mourning. How would the country come to terms with this great loss? The nation's armed forces were on full alert because of the possible outbreak of war. It was feared that America's enemies were behind the assassination. Even now they might seize this moment of weakness and take the opportunity to strike. No one knew why the president had been shot. Perhaps there were more killings to come.

Fortunately that was not to be the case. Americans stayed glued to their television sets for four days. They participated in the nation's grieving. Somehow the orderly rituals were a comfort that kept the country together. Lyndon Johnson knew he had a particularly tough job in the days ahead. It was a sad beginning for a man who had become president by accident.

Young Lyndon Johnson

Lyndon Baines Johnson was born on August 27, 1908, near Stonewall, in the hill country of central Texas. It was an area Johnson's ancestors had helped to settle. The night LBJ was born was a stormy one with winds that threatened to tear up trees by their roots. For three months the young child was nameless. His family called him Baby.

Johnson's birthplace was a ramshackle frame house with two rooms. The walls were full of holes. The bathroom was a two-seater outhouse. Both sets of Johnson's

The frame house where Lyndon Johnson was born

grandparents had been wealthy at one time, but lost their money in bad speculations. In 1908 the family was poor and felt the strain of rural poverty.

7

Lyndon's father, Sam Ealy Johnson, Jr., was a farmer and trader. He also became a member of the Texas State Legislature and served as an inspector for the Texas Railroad Commission. Sam Johnson's father was a Confederate army veteran who had also served in the Texas legislature.

Lyndon's mother was named Rebekah Baines. She was the daughter of an attorney who had moved to Texas in 1887 and invested in farmland. But his tenants failed to pay him and he went bankrupt.

Rebekah Baines was one of the few women in Texas at that time who was educated. She was a college graduate who taught elocution—effective public speaking—before her marriage to Sam Johnson. Lyndon was the eldest of the five Johnson children.

Because Lyndon's father and grandfather had been in politics, it was only natural that LBJ would follow them. Texas was a one-party state, and that party was the Democratic party. So it is not surprising that Lyndon grew up immersed in political talk. What's more, young Lyndon thoroughly enjoyed it.

Lyndon's father took the boy at a young age to San Antonio to see the Alamo. There he was profoundly impressed by the story of Texas heroism. Young Lyndon first tasted politics when his father ran for the Texas House of Representatives in 1918. Lyndon was nine and just finishing fifth grade. Both of these events made lasting impressions on the young boy. They contributed to his ambition to serve his country.

An early photo of young Lyndon

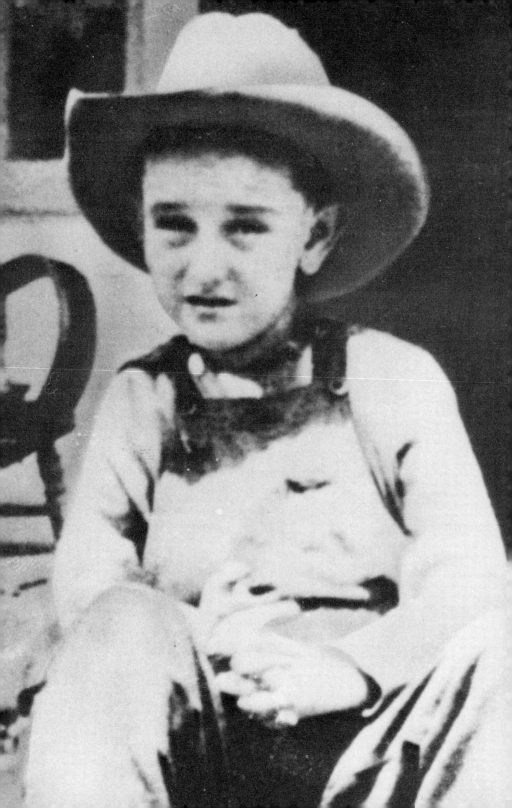

Lyndon went to high school in Johnson City and was an average scholar. He graduated at 15, but had no interest in going to college. Instead, beginning in 1924, he worked for two years at a variety of jobs. He shoveled rocks and he worked on a cotton gin. Bored, he went with some friends to California. There he picked grapes and washed dishes.

Then Johnson decided to give college a chance. Young Lyndon hitchhiked to San Marcos. There he worked his way through Southwest Texas State Teachers' College. First he was a janitor. Then he became an assistant to the president of the college.

Johnson had a college sweetheart named Carol Davis. She was the daughter of a wealthy Texas banker. The two planned to marry until Lyndon was invited to her parents' house one night for dinner. They thought he was boorish and self-centered.

They weren't alone in finding Lyndon Johnson rude and awkward. By now Johnson was six feet three inches tall and very skinny. He could be boastful and demanding. His college nickname was Bull. Even just out of college, Johnson was a man obsessed with ambition. A good friend said, "Something always seemed to be eating him."

Johnson's earliest teaching assignment was in a school for Hispanic students. Here Johnson learned firsthand about rural poverty while working among the children of agricultural workers who had recently immigrated from Mexico. He later taught speech and was the debate coach at Sam Houston High School in Houston.

Lyndon learned firsthand about poverty when he taught in rural schools. Here he poses with some fellow teachers.

In 1930 Lyndon Johnson got his first job in politics. He was invited to become secretary to Texas congressman Richard Kleberg. In 1931 he first made his way to Washington to work in Kleberg's office. With his customary speed, Johnson was on his way to a political career. It was a modest beginning, but it was a beginning.

Claudia Taylor

Claudia Alta Taylor was born in the eastern part of Texas, at Karnack, on December 22, 1912. Although she was christened Claudia, she was still an infant when a servant nicknamed her because she thought she was "purty as a ladybird." The name stuck and has followed Lady Bird all her life. It was the perfect name for the first lady who has been most closely associated with protecting the environment.

Lady Bird had been born into Texas wealth, but her mother died when the young girl was just five. She had two older brothers. Her father and aunt raised her. Mr. Taylor was a prosperous farmer and storekeeper.

Until she was 13, Lady Bird attended a one-room school. Then her father bought her a car so she could drive to high school. She went to St. Mary's Episcopal School for Girls in Dallas. Lady Bird then attended the University of Texas in Austin and graduated close to the top of her class with a Bachelor of Arts degree in 1933. She returned there the following year for a second degree, this time in journalism.

On November 17, 1934, LBJ married Lady Bird Taylor at St. Mark's Episcopal Church in San Antonio. Johnson was 26 and his wife was just 21. They had met earlier that same year in Austin. Johnson was spending most of his time in Washington working as Kleberg's secretary. Lady Bird found LBJ "the most outspoken, straightforward, determined young man" whom she had ever met.

One of the first photos that Lady Bird gave LBJ during their courtship   13

It was a whirlwind courtship and marriage. Johnson proposed to Lady Bird the day after their first date. They had breakfast in an Austin hotel and then went for a drive. Although Lady Bird did not accept his proposal that day, soon after she did. On the day of the wedding, just before the ceremony, the best man discovered that Lyndon had forgotten to provide a ring. He rushed across the street to a Sears Roebuck store and bought one that cost $2.50.

When marriage made Lady Bird's initials the same as her husband's, a family tradition began. To LBJ, however, Lady Bird was always "Bird." The Johnsons gave their two daughters names with the initials LBJ: Lynda Bird was born in March 1944, and Luci Baines was born in July 1947. The Johnsons had tried many times to have children, and Lady Bird had several miscarriages before 1944.

Early Politics

Johnson studied law briefly in 1934 at Washington's Georgetown University. But it seemed more and more that a life in politics was what Johnson most wanted. Johnson was ambitious and he was not a patient man. He wanted to become a powerful politician and a millionaire. In fact, Kleberg's wife wanted her husband to fire Johnson in 1935 because she thought Johnson was too ambitious.

Lyndon was a novice politician, but he was shrewd and a fast learner. He immersed himself in the world of Washington. He was also learning everything he could about Franklin Roosevelt's New Deal politics.

The Johnsons quickly settled into their small apartment in Washington. Because Lady Bird had grown up in wealth, she did not know how to prepare a meal or how to keep house. There is a story that Lady Bird needed a recipe to boil rice! But Lady Bird was almost as shrewd as her husband, and in a short time she was an excellent cook and housekeeper.

One of Roosevelt's agencies for helping to employ Americans (and thus bring an end to the depression) was the NYA, or National Youth Administration. In 1935 the agency was set up, and Johnson's good friend Sam Rayburn saw to it that Lyndon was named the administrator for the Texas office. The Johnsons even got to go back to their beloved Texas for a period.

Rayburn became one of the most influential figures in American politics. Lady Bird Johnson, in particular, charmed Rayburn. He called her "the greatest woman I have ever known." Rayburn was able to let Roosevelt know about the ambitious young Johnson. In 1940 Rayburn became Speaker of the House.

In 1937 Johnson really launched his political career. LBJ's father-in-law had loaned him $10,000. It was an advance from Lady Bird's inheritance from her mother. He made a bid for a seat in the House of Representatives as a New Deal politician, supporting Franklin D. Roosevelt. Johnson was successful and served in this office for five-and-one-half terms.

FDR supported LBJ in his political career, because Johnson supported his New Deal programs.

It was only after Johnson won his seat in the House that he actually met FDR. FDR liked Johnson's rough but volatile style and supported him strongly through his subsequent House of Representatives races. In both 1938 and 1940 Johnson won his seat with little if any opposition. In 1941 Johnson was defeated in a special election for the Senate, but he continued to serve in the House.

Lady Bird Johnson was a soft-spoken but hardworking political wife who hid enormous strength beneath her gentle exterior. She was always considered one of Johnson's strongest assets, especially when his career began to take on national importance. In 1942 Lady Bird worked in Lyndon's office. She answered correspondence, helped draft speeches and gave sightseeing tours of Washington, D.C., to visiting Texans.

When World War II broke out, LBJ volunteered for active duty in the navy. Because he had a seat on the Naval Affairs Committee, he instantly became a lieutenant commander. He received a Silver Star for his distinguished service in the South Pacific when he participated in a dangerous mission over New Guinea. His political career was interrupted during this time, but in 1942 Johnson returned to Washington and to the world of politics.

In 1943 Lady Bird Johnson bought a small radio station. She was able to do this with money she had inherited from her mother. While she ran it, the station made lots of money. Eventually the station became a huge money-maker for the whole family.

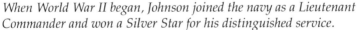

When World War II began, Johnson joined the navy as a Lieutenant Commander and won a Silver Star for his distinguished service.

The Senate by Age 40

Johnson was elected to the U.S. Senate in 1948. He was only 40 years old. Johnson defeated his opponent, Coke Stevenson, by a mere 87 votes. There were unkind hints of "dirty" Texas politics. Johnson was called Landslide Lyndon by some of his enemies—and his friends. Truman's Fair Deal had replaced Roosevelt's New Deal, and Johnson opposed some of Truman's measures.

As a senator, Johnson worked long days and late hours. Neither he nor Lady Bird had much time to take advantage of Washington's political or social life. They were simply too busy. What little time they did have they wanted to spend in Texas.

In 1951 the Johnsons bought the land and house that would become known as the LBJ Ranch. The house had been built by Johnson's grandparents. He bought the house from an aunt. Situated about 15 miles from Johnson City, the house grew to 13 rooms by the time renovations were complete. The Johnsons made improvements to the stone house with two-foot-thick walls. They added five rooms to the original building. There are verandas and porches all around the rambling house, which sits on some 400 acres. The Johnsons raised cattle there. After Johnson became president, the ranch became known as the Texas White House.

In 1951 Johnson took another step up the political ladder. He was given an important senatorial spot as majority whip. The whip directs all the senators of his party and makes sure they are around when they are needed. Although the job is not a powerful one, it requires organization, which Johnson had in abundance. He acted quickly and he got results. And people liked those qualities.

In 1953 he became Senate minority leader. In 1952 the Republican candidate, Dwight Eisenhower, had won the election as president. At the same time the Republican Party won a majority of the Senate seats. Even though he was a Democrat, Johnson offered support to President Eisenhower. He was able to help secure passage of a number of Eisenhower initiatives.

In the 1954 election Democratic legislators gained control in Congress. In 1955 Johnson became majority leader. At 47 he was the youngest majority leader in history. Even though Congress had shifted to a Democratic majority, LBJ pushed a number of Eisenhower's proposals through the Democrat-controlled Congress. This showed his consummate skill as a politician. He was always loyal to his party, yet he was able to obtain cooperation from leaders in both parties. He was able to keep good relations with most people.

During the early 1950s Republican senator Joseph McCarthy of Wisconsin was making himself greatly feared by denouncing many Americans as Communists. Johnson was able to use his influence to censure McCarthy.

Johnson suffered a serious heart attack in July 1955, just months after becoming majority leader. He spent five weeks in the hospital and then returned to his ranch to recuperate. At this time he gave up a three-pack-a-day cigarette habit. He was out of action through January 1956. Although the illness waylaid him for more than half a year, he came back fitter than ever and more capable of doing important things.

As Vice President

Johnson had hoped to run for president in 1960. He and his advisers had even quietly begun a campaign program. But public attention now focused on a new-style politician, John Fitzgerald Kennedy. His youth, his style and his charm captivated Democrats as well as other Americans. Suddenly Kennedy looked like a new American hero.

So Lyndon Johnson had no chance at the presidency in 1960. Kennedy was nominated on the first ballot at the Democratic convention in July. Kennedy asked Johnson to be his running mate. The vice presidential role did not appeal to Johnson's ego, but he accepted. Although his heart attack had occurred only five years earlier, he still kept up a furious pace. Perhaps being vice president was a sensible alternative to his ambition. Certainly it pleased Lady Bird.

The move was also a shrewd one on Kennedy's part. Kennedy—a New Englander—desperately needed to woo southern voters, and in this way Johnson was a distinct asset. No sooner had Johnson agreed to run than he went barnstorming through the South, looking for any votes he could muster for the ticket.

Lyndon Johnson fit the pattern of the southern Democrat—gracious and with a conservative and paternalistic regard for tradition. He stood for the privileges of wealth and the landed aristocracy, but he also had strong liberal political leanings.

Johnson proved to be an able vice president. Here President Kennedy gives a warm handshake to LBJ on the White House grounds.

The 1960 election put the Kennedy-Johnson ticket into the White House, but only narrowly. Perhaps the nation as a whole wasn't as eager for Kennedy as were most of the Democratic liberals.

While Johnson was vice president, his relations with Kennedy's advisers were not especially cordial. The Kennedy men—a new breed of liberals—did not like Johnson or his team. Johnson mistrusted the eastern Ivy League intellectuals with whom Kennedy surrounded himself. But the public was scarcely aware of any ill will. The political backbiting was kept out of the press. The irony, of course, was that Johnson had far more political experience than anyone on the Kennedy team.

During his vice presidency Johnson did the usual things a vice president does. He was chair of several committees and made 11 overseas trips on behalf of the United States. On one of these trips in 1961, he visited West Berlin and was able to assert the American position there. He was also active in supporting the growing space program, an interest that dated back to Johnson's Senate days.

The First 30 Days

Suddenly, with Kennedy's death, Johnson was thrust into a new role. Johnson was in shock as he replaced Kennedy. But then so was the whole nation. Only with Lincoln's assassination almost 100 years earlier had the nation felt a loss so strongly.

In his book, *The Vantage Point*, Johnson recalled his thoughts on the day of Kennedy's death, as he sped from Parkland Hospital to Love Field. "I had to convince everyone everywhere that the country would go forward, that the business of the United States would proceed."

Johnson wisely spent the first few days getting a firm grasp on the situation. He studied reports. He contacted people the world over. He spoke with Kennedy family members, key politicians and world leaders. He needed to keep Kennedy staffers in their jobs. He would need the help of all these people.

Johnson was a dynamo. It has been said that in his first 30 days as president, Johnson spoke with more than 3,000 people and averaged no more than four to five hours of sleep a night. Johnson had a reputation for using the telephone a great deal. His telephone had 42 separate lines. Some people have said that he spent more time talking on the phone than any other president.

The new president moved with his customary speed. Johnson's first maneuvers as president were to carry forward the programs on which Kennedy had been working at the time of his death. These measures included a tax cut and a new civil rights bill. Within two days of Kennedy's burial, Johnson had managed to slash $5 million from the federal budget. Johnson's skilled handling of many of the details of governing the country was largely due to his excellent advisers. Together they helped the nation weather a potentially bad time. The country emerged stronger and more unified.

Johnson developed the War on Poverty program. As early as 1964 he was able to see the Economic Opportunities Act passed. This created several antipoverty programs to help the poor and out of work.

With old business taken care of, Johnson moved on to his plan "to build a great society, a place where the meaning of man's life matches the marvels of man's labors." He wanted life to be more satisfying and enriching for all Americans.

Kennedy had been greatly hampered in his attempts to bring about social change. This was largely because Congress resisted his efforts to bring about desired legislation. But Johnson was able to use his skills to obtain passage of one of the most sweeping legislative programs in American history.

Always the crafty politician, Johnson was able to draw on a backlog of obligations built up through decades of political favors. He used persuasion and political pressure to see social legislation, welfare reform and health and education programs passed by Congress.

Seated at his desk, Johnson signs the Civil Rights Bill as Martin Luther King, Jr., looks on.

The Johnson White House

The only change Johnson made to the Oval Office he inherited from President Kennedy was to order a new—and larger—rocking chair. Johnson had TV consoles with three screens placed both upstairs and in his office downstairs so he could watch media coverage on all the major television networks. These were operated by remote control. There were also push-button dispensers for soda and coffee.

Johnson's White House bedroom was a duplicate of his bedroom at the LBJ Ranch back in Texas. He had a superstrong showerhead installed in his private bathroom because he found it invigorating.

The Johnsons enjoyed entertaining in a friendly and relaxed way. This was in contrast to the Kennedys, who were more sophisticated and formal in their lifestyle.

The Johnsons often informally entertained many prominent—and some not so prominent—figures. Once they held a county fair on the lawn for the children of congressmembers. Their most popular type of get-together was, not surprisingly, the Texas barbecue. Frequent cookouts occurred on the White House third-floor roof, where an elaborate barbecue complex had been set up. The Texas influence was felt in the menus: black-eyed peas, deer sausage, charbroiled steak and barbecued ribs. During many of the Johnson social functions, dancing was a featured activity.

Lady Bird Johnson relied heavily on her social secretary, Bess Abell. Abell was one of the first social secretaries to assume major importance in the day-to-day running of the White House. On occasion she even acted as Lady Bird's assistant hostess.

Christmas was an important time for the Johnsons. Mrs. Johnson said Christmases at the White House "have been touched by the continuity of tradition and the mood of the time." Christmas was so much a family tradition that the Johnsons celebrated only two of their six White House Christmases in Washington. The others were spent at home on their Texas ranch.

Lynda Johnson and her younger sister Luci (left) *play with one of the family beagles in this picture taken about 1964.*

In 1963 Luci Johnson was enjoying a holiday fire in her second-floor bedroom fireplace. The fire blazed out of control and sent billows of smoke into the room. The plucky girl put out the fire herself with glasses of water from the bathroom. She then tried to keep it a secret from her father.

Lady Bird Johnson carried on Jackie Kennedy's plans for the interior decoration of the White House. Shortly after her husband's assassination, Mrs. Kennedy had told Mrs. Johnson, "Don't be frightened of this house. . . . Some of the happiest years of my marriage have been spent here—you will be happy here."

In 1964 President Johnson created the Committee for the Preservation of the White House. At the same time he established the permanent post of White House curator. "My respect for this great old house grows day by day. I want to leave it a little richer." She continued Jackie Kennedy's plans, working with curator Jim Ketchum. In 1965 Lady Bird dedicated the Jacqueline Kennedy Garden in her honor.

The Johnsons were able to add several important paintings to the permanent White House collection. Mrs. Johnson also acquired a genuine 18th-century crèche (nativity scene) for the White House. She had sent a representative to purchase it in Italy. It is a remarkable crèche and has joined the many valuable treasures that make up the White House collection.

First Family

Lady Bird Johnson was described by her press secretary as "a woman who listens." Lady Bird was always seen as a warm, interested and caring woman who was able to be both a public and private person. She was a first lady and a mother and, always, wife to both the private and public LBJ.

Lynda was 19 when her father became president and Luci was just 16. Both were growing up in the public eye. The sisters were very sensitive to living in the White House fishbowl. Their every date and every new dress was seized upon by the press and made into a major news event. Lynda was a student at George Washington University, majoring in history. Luci attended the National Cathedral School in nearby Georgetown. Secret Service agents accompanied them to school and sat with them in their classes. The agents even accompanied the girls and their escorts on dates around town.

The solarium was the Johnson girls' salvation. This was the same sunny room that had been Caroline Kennedy's nursery school. The Johnsons turned it into a recreation room where both girls could entertain their dates without their Secret Service chaperones. Here they also played bridge, danced and held parties.

With the help of designers, Lady Bird put her personal stamp on a few rooms in the upstairs private living quarters. These rooms included her own bedroom and dressing rooms and her daughters' rooms. Both Lynda and Luci helped their mother decorate the family sitting room.

Mrs. Johnson's decorating scheme for the living quarters made use of her favorite colors, lemon yellow and lime green. Even then she favored the environmental "green" that would later occupy so much of her energy.

During her time in the White House, Mrs. Johnson began a program for the beautification of much of the area surrounding the White House. As first lady, Lady Bird traveled 200,000 miles to improve the landscape of America. The 1965 Highway Act restricted placement of billboards and roadside junkyards. It was part of her overall program to keep America beautiful.

One of Lady Bird's favorite sports was bowling. At that time the White House's recreational facilities included an underground bowling alley. She felt the game was a wonderful way to release the tensions that were part of life in the public eye.

The Johnsons loved animals and LBJ kept beagles most of his life. When the Johnsons came to the White House, they brought a pair, Him and Her. In 1964 Johnson picked up both dogs by their ears. News photographers latched on to this, and much of America was outraged. Both dogs died when they were young and were replaced by a mongrel named Yuki.

Yuki wanted to play a part in Luci's wedding by being included in the formal wedding photograph. But Mrs. Johnson put her foot down and Yuki is absent from the family pictures. Stories circulated that many of the Johnsons' dogs were not housebroken. As Johnson's popularity with the American public waned, he turned more and more to his canine friends for support.

The family was often troubled by the protest movements that became a way of life in the 1960s. Noisy demonstrations near the White House against LBJ and U.S. involvement in the Vietnam War often kept the family awake at night. The Johnson daughters remember catching glimpses of their father working late at night. He was slumped over papers spread on the dining room table in the private living quarters. He was deeply troubled by the country's unrest.

When Johnson picked up his dogs by the ears, many Americans were upset. Johnson insisted that it didn't hurt them.

Johnson shakes hands with the people at a stop during his campaign tour of the country by train.

President in His Own Right

Whatever Johnson did between November 1963 and the following summer struck people as fine. In August 1964 he was named by the Democrats as their presidential candidate for the upcoming election. His running mate was the Minnesota senator Hubert H. Humphrey.

During the campaign the candidates used a ten-car train that also carried Mrs. Johnson across the country. Along with their advisers and supporters, the Johnsons made stops in many states and stirred up voters.

In the November election Johnson and Humphrey ran against Republican Barry Goldwater. Goldwater was a right-wing extremist who stood little chance of a good showing. Johnson carried the popular vote by more than 60 percent. He also won 486 electoral votes, more than anyone since Roosevelt's 1936 election. More than 90 percent of black voters supported Johnson. Most important of all, Johnson had won the presidency on his own terms.

Lyndon Johnson's only inauguration occurred on January 20, 1965. After the ceremony the Johnsons were driven from the Capitol down Pennsylvania Avenue to the White House. From a reviewing stand there they watched the bands and festivities. During part of the day, Him, one of Johnson's beagles, sat with the family.

That night the Johnsons attended five different inaugural balls. At each the first couple stopped in just long enough to greet old friends and to dance briefly.

The Johnson
Weddings

Both Johnson daughters were married while their father was president. Lyndon Johnson was only the second person to give away two daughters while president. Woodrow Wilson had been the first.

Luci was married in 1966 to Patrick J. Nugent. Earlier her engagement to the ex-serviceman had made the expected headlines. The ceremony was held on August 6. Patrick was 23 years old and Luci was just 19. Luci became a Roman Catholic in order to marry Nugent. The couple was married at the immense National Shrine of the Immaculate Conception in Washington. The basilica is a huge building of marble and gleaming mosaics. Luci's sister, Lynda, was her maid of honor. Luci had ten bridesmaids, all dressed in pink taffeta. The hem of each gown was embroidered with Luci's name and the date.

The reception took place at the White House. The Nugents greeted guests in a receiving line in the Blue Room. There the first White House wedding had taken place 146 years earlier when James Monroe's daughter, Maria, had been married.

The reception itself took place in the East Room. The room was elegantly decorated with flowers. The wedding cake stood eight feet tall and weighed 300 pounds.

The Nugents honeymooned in the Bahamas. For privacy they traveled under the assumed name of Mr. and Mrs. Frisbee. Later they settled in Austin, Texas.

Maybe the fact that Lynda caught her sister's bouquet had something to do with her good fortune. For a while Lynda had dated the Hollywood actor George Hamilton. Then, even more than ever, her activities made headlines. But on December 9, 1967, Lynda Bird Johnson was married to marine officer Charles S. Robb, then 28.

President Johnson adjusts the wedding gown of his daughter Lynda after her marriage to Charles Robb.

This time both the ceremony and the reception were held at the White House. The ceremony took place in the East Room, where both Wilson daughters had been wed. The East Room was decorated with greenery and tiny white lights that twinkled. Lynda wore a white satin gown embroidered with pearls. Luci was her sister's matron of honor.

Lynda's wedding was somewhat less elaborate than Luci's had been. Still, on this occasion more than 500 press and media staff members were present. There were also another 500 invited guests, many of whom were prominent figures from the worlds of politics and entertainment.

Theodore Roosevelt's daughter attended the wedding. Alice Roosevelt Longworth, then 83, said, "I've never been to a wedding as pretty as this." She herself had been married at the White House in 1906.

But the shadow of Vietnam hung over Lynda's wedding. The groom left for Vietnam a few months after the wedding. His best man, an army captain, had just returned from the conflict a few days before the ceremony.

The first Johnson grandchild, Patrick Lyndon Nugent, was born in July 1967. The infant was a frequent visitor to the White House. His proud grandfather carried him to state dinners and formal receptions, introducing him to world leaders and other distinguished guests.

The Robb marriage has endured, but the Nugents were divorced in 1979. Luci later married Ian Turpin and the couple divide their time between Austin, Texas, and Toronto, Canada.

The Johnson Era

In the 1960s America was finding itself, and people were expressing themselves in new ways. This was the period of "hootenannies"—These were gatherings of people who performed folk songs, traditional American dances and sing-a-longs. It was a time when a real sense of culture began to emerge in America. It was a time of celebration of America's contributions to the arts.

Along with America's new interest in culture came a recognition of the nation's beauty—and the need to protect it. Around the country billboards came down. With tougher legislation people began to make a real effort not to litter. Laws were passed that encouraged urban planning. Cities would no longer happen haphazardly. As first lady, Lady Bird Johnson believed in this planning. She worked hard for her favorite causes.

Lyndon Johnson also worked hard. He drove himself endlessly. But he also played as hard as he worked. Legends tell of hair-raising limousine rides on the LBJ Ranch. There are other stories, too. Rich men are often cheap, and Johnson was no exception. He waged war against keeping all the lights on in the White House. He often went from room to room turning off the light switches. It seemed to make sense to him to save a little money here and there. Some of his "friends" in the press dubbed him Lightbulb Lyndon.

Johnson also upset Secret Service guards because he was so swift. Frequently they had to rescue him from crowds outside the gates to the White House grounds. Often he went there just to chat with his fellow Americans.

More and more, though, Johnson could not go out among his fellow Americans. They had begun to hold him responsible for the Vietnam War. As a result he remained in the White House, isolated from the common people.

A Time of Protest

Public protesting became a way of life during Johnson's presidency. Civil rights was one of the issues about which Americans protested.

Johnson addressed Congress in 1963, in the first speech given there by a president since 1946. Both Mrs. Johnson and Lynda were there to hear Johnson ask for the National Guard to be called out in Alabama. He felt they were needed to protect the civil rights marchers there.

In 1965 the Reverend Martin Luther King, Jr., led a group of blacks and whites into Selma, Alabama. They were there to demand the right to register to vote. People there viciously attacked the marchers.

On August 6, 1965, the Voting Rights Act was signed. The legislation represents one of the high points of Johnson's career. It was also the most sweeping piece of civil rights legislation in 100 years.

Also in 1965 Johnson was called upon to prevent the revolution in the Dominican Republic from turning into a Communist takeover. Then in 1967 the Israelis and Arabs launched a deadly war in the Middle East. It lasted only six days, but it had repercussions that are still being felt. At home, rioting in largely black neighborhoods in Newark,

Johnson works late in the Cabinet Room. The 1960s was a time of many crises and the president had to deal with most of them.

New Jersey, and Detroit, Michigan, caused some anxiety. On all fronts Johnson was beset by problems.

During Johnson's term in office, Martin Luther King, Jr., was assassinated in April of 1968. The event again touched off rioting in many cities, and Washington, D.C., was no exception. In fact, there was violence within a few blocks of the White House, and troops were sent in, just in case.

John F. Kennedy's brother, Robert Kennedy, was killed in Los Angeles in June 1968, during meetings leading up to the Democratic party convention.

Johnson weathered all these trials. After all, he had kept the nation together after the Kennedy assassination. He had pushed through a great deal of legislation during a period of untold prosperity. But by 1968 the Great Society seemed a far-off dream. It had been pushed into the background. Another problem had become more important to Americans.

The War in Vietnam

The war in Vietnam was not a creation of Lyndon Johnson's presidency. The problems in Southeast Asia had gone back at least as far as Eisenhower and Kennedy. Even while Harry Truman was president, the United States had expressed a commitment to keeping communism from spreading throughout the world.

The French had formerly controlled Vietnam—or Indochina, as it was then called. But they had given up the fight: North Vietnam was Communist, while South Vietnam was not. The United States felt it should pick up where the French government had left off in keeping South Vietnam free.

By 1962 there were some 11,000 U.S. military personnel stationed in Vietnam. They were described as "advisers." In 1963 Kennedy ordered more than 16,000 troops into the country. It seemed the wisest course of action to take. As vice president, Johnson backed Kennedy's actions.

After Johnson became president, he sent American planes to bomb North Vietnam. This was done to support the South Vietnamese. They were still struggling to resist the threat from the Communist North. Suddenly the North Vietnamese were making retaliatory strikes against U.S. ships off the coast of North Vietnam, in the Tonkin Gulf. The Tonkin Gulf Resolution was passed in order to allow the United States to protect its forces there. By the end of 1964 there were some 190,000 U.S. troops in South Vietnam.

Back home, people were not able to understand what was going on or why it was happening. There began a great split in the United States between those who supported the

A crowd of American soldiers greets President Johnson during his visit to Vietnam.

war and those who opposed it. Johnson, his advisers and the military were called warmongers or hawks. Those who favored peace—at any price—were called doves.

As the war continued to escalate, more and more soldiers were being forced to go overseas to fight for something very far removed from their understanding. How could a tiny, undeveloped country on the other side of the world be of importance? Every time a soldier went—or the fighting escalated—the cost of the war went up. For the first time in history, a large number of Americans seriously questioned the moral correctness of what was being done by the United States government.

In early 1968 the Tet offensive was launched. North Vietnam began a particularly brutal attack on the South. Now there were more than 600,000 Americans fighting in Vietnam. And the costs were outrageous, both in dollars and in human lives. Many Americans were beginning to lose respect for their government and for the president.

The young, in particular, were making themselves heard. On many campuses there were sit-ins, teach-ins, building takeovers and hostage situations. Ordinary students—not just politically active ones—were getting involved. Campus protests in the spring of 1968 were noisy and potentially dangerous. Soldiers were dying in Vietnam at the rate of 100 a month. Something had to happen.

On March 31, 1968, Johnson made a speech to the nation. The talk was to give the American public news about the Tet offensive, but at the end of his speech, Johnson also announced that he would not seek reelection that fall. He stated that he wanted to devote all his time to ending the Vietnam conflict once and for all. He would seek negotiations to end the bombing in Vietnam. It was an honest and useful suggestion. What he didn't say was that his popularity was at such a low ebb that there was little chance he would be able to win the upcoming election.

His face worn by the pressures of his office, Johnson announces to the American people that he will neither seek nor accept his party's nomination for president.

After the White House, Johnson removed himself from politics and ran his Texas ranch.

After the White House

Johnson's successor, Richard M. Nixon, ran on a Republican platform that promised to put an end to the Vietnam War. But it took until Nixon's second term for him to make good on that promise.

On January 20, 1969, the Johnsons left the White House for the last time. That day they had attended the inauguration of the newly elected president, Richard M. Nixon. The Johnsons welcomed the new first family and then returned directly to their ranch in Texas.

When his time at the White House was over, Johnson looked forward to retiring with Lady Bird to their Texas ranch. There he worked on his memoirs and ran the affairs of the ranch. Johnson had effectively removed himself from the political arena. He had said he was going to the ranch to "read, write and loaf." And that, by his own choice, is exactly what he did.

Johnson endowed two buildings in Austin at the University of Texas. These include the LBJ School of Public Affairs and the Lyndon Baines Johnson Presidential Library and Museum. The library stands eight stories tall and contains some 31 million pages of documents. It was opened and dedicated in 1971.

In January of 1973 Johnson was napping at his ranch when he suffered another massive heart attack. This time he was not so lucky and died en route to a hospital.

Johnson's body was flown to Washington, D.C. There the body lay in state in the Capitol rotunda. After the funeral in Washington, Johnson's remains were returned to Texas. There he was buried in a family plot among the oak

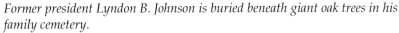

Former president Lyndon B. Johnson is buried beneath giant oak trees in his family cemetery.

trees with his parents and grandparents. Nearby stand his beloved LBJ Ranch and the banks of the Pedernales River. It is a part of the world that Johnson loved very much.

Johnson was a wealthy man. He came to the White House with about $14 million in assets. When he died, he was the wealthiest ex-president the country had ever known. By then his fortune had grown to more than $20 million.

After Johnson's death Lady Bird suffered a temporary decline in her own health and vigor. By the year's end, however, she had snapped out of it. Once again she threw herself into her favorite projects. In 1983 she founded the National Wildflower Research Center.

Lady Bird Johnson turned 80 in 1992. Today she is still a hard worker. She continues her interest in the environment and in keeping the American landscape beautiful.

The Johnson Legacy

Johnson had a dream of a Great Society for all Americans and all people of the world. In trying to achieve it, he presided over one of the most sweeping legislative programs in history. Abroad he maintained the image of a powerful America through continuation of the Cold War. He watched the Communist onslaught in Vietnam escalate. He retaliated by sending troops and military aid to the beleaguered country.

Some have seen Johnson as a political opportunist. Some have even tried to implicate him in the assassination of John F. Kennedy, primarily because he was the prime beneficiary of Lee Harvey Oswald, Kennedy's killer. LBJ was the person who most directly benefited by the beloved president's death, inheriting the full power and prestige of the nation's highest office.

Lady Bird Johnson—usually at her husband's side—was a serene and controlled personality. Underneath her calm exterior Lady Bird had enormous power on important issues. She almost always managed to get her own way—by convincing others sweetly and serenely that her way was the best.

LBJ was known to have a stormy, fiery temper. He was easily provoked, but the anger just as quickly disappeared. Lady Bird could say a great deal with just a look or one sharp word. Her daughters said they never saw her lose control.

The Johnsons were relaxed, friendly people, and their lives reflected this. Their two young daughters tried to lead normal lives in the White House. But because of them, as well as the expected political activity of the nation's first family, the White House was always lively.

LBJ understood power and the use of power. This is one of the things that made him an effective president. When he went into the Senate, he made it his business to learn everything. No member of Congress ever knew more about the way Congress works. When he became president, he applied the same rules to that office.

Like the state of Texas that he loved so much, LBJ was larger than life. He was first and foremost a politician. And he was a good and shrewd one. As such—and despite Vietnam—he was one of the most successful presidents of the 20th century.

For Further Reading

Anthony, Carl Sferrazza. *First Ladies: The Saga of the Presidents' Wives and Their Power, 1789-1961*. New York: William Morrow and Company, Inc., 1990.

Conkin, Paul K. *Big Daddy from the Pedernales*. Boston: Twayne Publishers, A Division of G. K. Hall and Co., 1986.

Falkof, Lucille. *Lyndon B. Johnson: 36th President of the United States*. Ada, Oklahoma: Garrett Educational Corporation, 1989.

Fisher, Leonard Everett. *The White House*. New York: Holiday House, 1989.

Friedel, Frank. *The Presidents of the United States of America*. Revised edition. Washington, D.C.: The White House Historical Association, 1989.

Gould, Lewis L. *Lady Bird Johnson and the Environment*. Lawrence, Kansas: The University of Kansas Press, 1988.

Johnson, Lady Bird. *White House Diary*. New York: Holt, Rinehart and Winston, 1970.

Klapthor, Margaret Brown. *The First Ladies*. Revised edition. Washington, D.C.: The White House Historical Association, 1989.

Lindsay, Rae. *The Presidents' First Ladies*. New York: Franklin Watts, 1989.

The Living White House. Revised edition. Washington, D.C.: The White House Historical Association, 1987.

Menendez, Albert J. *Christmas in the White House*. Philadelphia: The Westminster Press, 1983.

St. George, Judith. *The White House: Cornerstone of a Nation*. New York: G. P. Putnam's Sons, 1990.

Sandak, Cass R. *The White House*. New York: Franklin Watts, 1980.

Taylor, Tim. *The Book of Presidents*. New York: Arno Press, A New York Times Company, 1972.

The White House. Washington, D.C.: The White House Historical Association, 1987.

Index

48